Lessons From Divorce

From Tragedy to Triumph

Venisha Terrae Jackson

ISBN#: 979-8-87271-868-0

Library of Congress Cataloging in-Publication Data

First Printing April 2024
Printed in the U.S.A.

Foreword

Ever since I was a little girl, I wanted to become a wife. As I was growing up, I watched, admired, and looked up to my grandmother Mordester Jackson. She was some kind of woman. Not only was she a mother, but she was also a woman of faith, a prayer warrior, a sister and friend to many and her smile was contagious. Grandma, as I affectionately called her, was everything I aspired to become. She taught me life lessons that I still apply in my life today.

My desire of becoming a wife finally came to fruition, but on February 20, 2022 it was dissolved and I will never forget lying in bed and asking God how and why I ended up here. I heard Him say to me so clearly, *"Learn the Lessons."* At that moment, my ears opened, and my sense of discernment became keener. When things transpired throughout my divorce process, I no longer asked God why, but I began to ask, "What's the Lesson?"

This book has been written to help those who are dealing with the stain of divorce to know and understand that there is still life on the other side of divorce. I still believe in the institution of marriage and love.

I dedicate this book to everyone who has felt the sting of divorce and the grief that it brings. To every person who struggles with the question, "will I survive this?" …the answer is YES you will. I dedicate this book to the woman that I am growing to be. It was because of these lessons that I am able to testify that you can indeed go from 'Tragedy to Triumph'. I can boldly declare as the Psalmist did in Psalm 34:4 "I sought the Lord and he heard me and delivered me from all of my fears."

Acknowledgements

I give God glory, honor, and praise for the ability to survive one of the worst seasons of my life. I'm also thankful for my family. So many people stood by me throughout that process, and I am grateful that I am on the other side.

To my biological mother Carolyn Faye and Helen Ann, my "auntie-mom" as I affectionately call her, you both have seen me and loved me through a variety of seasons. I am grateful for your love and support. I have learned as I get older, that "family" is not always those who carry the same DNA as you.

Some people come into our lives and are ordained by God to help catapult us, love us, teach us, and support us and I will never discount those people. To my God Parents Apostle Cary L. and Lady Brenda D. Baker. You both listened to me beg and cry for God to send me a husband and you've been there when I cried because it had ended. You opened your home and your resources to ensure that I had an opportunity for a fresh start. You've been good to me and I will NEVER forget it. Thank you for loving and caring for me as your own. I will forever be your "Dimple Darling Baby."

I want to acknowledge and thank my Pastor and First Lady who covered me during the roughest, toughest season of my life Superintendent Earnest L. and Lady Jascena Sweat. Pastor and Lady Sweat you both suffered with me. You prayed me out of the pits of hell and loved me, encouraged me, and NEVER EVER changed with me. Thank you for being who you both are in the kingdom.

"My Bishop" Bishop Robert G. and "My Lady Mae" Lady Michelle Rudolph, thank you both for your consistent love, care, and concern and for not ever changing. I love you both for real!

My Sister Friends: Tiffany Barnes, Marcia Strickland, Hope Carey, Patience Carey, and Kymala Calloway, each of you showed up for me in ways unimaginable. I appreciate the authentic sisterhood!

To my Texas Crew: Cousin Tauna, My sisters Ranisha, Sharon, and LaChanda, each of you served your time with me during that season and some are still doing time. I love each of you!

To my dock partner: you pushed me. You encouraged me. You asked me almost every day, "Did you write today?" You are such a breath of fresh air! Meeting you was not by chance. God does ALL things well. In life, it's not where you go but who goes with you. Thank you for walking this journey with me. I will always be, "Your V. Jack".

Introduction

In 'Lessons From Divorce' the author delves into the profound impact of divorce, which is a time that can lead to devastation, not only for the two individuals involved, but also for the children, family, and friends. Yet, amidst the turmoil, there lies a glimmer of hope. There is life after divorce. In this book, the author explores this journey of transformation, drawing from her personal experience.

Through ten invaluable lessons, she offers insights and guidance for navigating the complexities of divorce, ultimately revealing that joy and renewal can emerge on the other side and one can go from despair to empowerment. The book offers hope and inspiration for those navigating the tumultuous aftermath of divorce. Through faith and introspection, she found solace in God's presence, realizing that He alone can heal the wounds and guide all who go through the difficulties and pain of divorce towards true happiness. This poignant narrative offers hope and inspiration for those navigating the tumultuous aftermath of divorce.

Contents

Lesson 1

Your Dependency is on God

"Therefore take no thought, saying, what shall we eat? Or, What shall we drink? Or, wherewithal shall we be clothed? For after all these things do the Gentiles seek? For your heavenly Father knoweth that ye have need of things." ~Matthew 6: 31-34.

I had always wanted to be a wife to a good man and when I finally got married, it was for better or for worse, in sickness and in health. In my heart and mind, I took my vows seriously. Divorce was something that I had never envisioned, so when it happened, I was devastated. The fact that I initiated the divorce did not diminish the hurt and devastation I felt over the loss of my marriage. I married for better for worse, but not better or worst. When two people marry, it should be because they love each other and want to spend the rest of their lives together. They do not go into the marriage thinking that they would eventually end up in divorce.

When I met my husband, I had just come out of a relationship that had depleted me mentally and psychologically. I had given so much of myself and I felt that I had also lost much of myself. I had made the decision that I was going to take the time to heal and focus on myself, so I spent my days working and self-reflecting. Many days I would journal and pray and as the Holy Spirit revealed to me, the areas that needed work in, so I committed myself to doing the work. Day by day, I was getting better.

I was working in the hotel industry at the time, and one of my coworkers, a very sweet lady who was saved began telling me about the church that she was attending. She knew that I hadn't been to church in some months, and she invited me to come. I was hesitant about going at first because at that time, I was over church. I was a little disappointed with God at that time because of the hurt and the pain that I was experiencing, but after much self-reflection and realization, I came to the conclusion that I would have never had to experience those things had I just consulted with God first.

I agreed to go to the evening service with her and I thoroughly enjoyed the worship experience and the Word; so much so, that I went back the following Sunday for the morning service. That next Sunday, I sat in the center section of the church, and I felt something that I had not felt in a long time. It was the Holy Spirit wrapping His arms around me. The name of the church was Temple of Restoration. God spoke to me that morning and told me that he was going to restore me there. At end of the service, an appeal was made, and I knew that I needed to connect to a body of believers so that God could finish the work that He had started in me. Needless to say, I joined the church. It was in the new members orientation class that I had my first encounter with my soon-to-be husband. He had just joined the church a few weeks prior to me. In the new members class, he sat next to the pastor, and they were always laughing and joking in class, which aggravated me at first because I am a serious person and didn't find anything funny. While in class, he and the pastor affectionately called me "Evangelist." During one of the classes, he decided to change his seat to come and sit next to me. I said to him, "Don't sit next to me. Go back and sit next to the pastor." The entire class laughed. His response was, "I am going to sit right here." …and he never moved.

As time went on, I informed the Pastor that I was not going to make it to church one Sunday because I did not have a ride. He told me that he would send someone to get me. And yes, he sent "J". When he rang my doorbell and I saw that it was him, I was livid. I wondered why the Pastor would send a male to pick me up. We talked on the way to church and then exchanged numbers. As time went by, J and I would talk periodically. One day, as I was driving home from Mississippi coming from my uncle's funeral, I got a call from J. inviting me to his mother's church. At the time, he was pursuing licensure in the Church of God in Christ as an Elder and would be preaching his trial sermon there, and I agreed to go. He shared that another couple would be going with us. The couple thought that we were dating, but I kept telling them that we were just friends. The next day we all drove to Crossett, Arkansas to support him for his trial sermon. As he was preaching in the church, I blurted out (without thinking) "Preach Baby." Immediately, I grabbed my mouth because I could not believe what had just come out of it. The lady who had ridden down with us started laughing so hard. She was recording him, so she had me on the recording. On the way back home, she played it back and we laughed for hours. There was something in me that knew he was going to be my husband. I felt like he was the one that God had for me. When we made it back to Little Rock, the couple let us know that they were planning a get-together on Christmas Eve for couples, and they wanted us to come. I said, "We aren't a couple", but they insisted, and we agreed to come. When Christmas Eve came, we went to the couple's house and had a good time. After the night ended, he drove me home - the long way. We talked and laughed, and the rest was history.

As time progressed, so did our relationship. We were getting very close, so one day I asked him why he was in my life. I was used to the games that guys played and at that point in my life I was not interested in being a part of the shenanigans, so I told him to be upfront and straightforward with me. If it was sex that he wanted, to say that; if he just wanted friendship and nothing serious, to say that too. All I asked was for him to be straightforward with me. He looked me in my eyes and said, *"Venisha, I want you and I am here to stay.* "Time went on and we often had in depth conversations about various things, including marriage. One day while sitting in the living room, he asked me if I would marry him. I said "yes." He then said, but I do not have a ring. I said, "I would still marry you." The ring was just an outward declaration for others. He asked me again that same year in October and this time he had a ring.

We got married that following March. It rained so hard on our wedding day, and I was a nervous wreck. I wanted everything to go as smoothly as smooth as possible and it did. It was a beautiful day. …But Marriage begins when the ceremony is over. When all the guests ae gone home, and all that is left is you and your spouse, that's when the real work begins. The two becoming one flesh is hard. My husband and I had very different personalities. It was very rare that we saw things from the same lens. That's what made us unique. And like every other marriage, we endured hardships, setbacks and disappointments, but we worked them out together. I literally lived out the majority of my wedding vows with him. We had some good days, better days, and worse days. We ministered to each other in times of sickness and in health. Unfortunately, we didn't make it to death do us part. Devastating circumstances caused us to part.

Just before my life was turned upside down, I had a good job, had just moved into a beautiful home and felt that life was good, but when the reality hit that I was divorced after ten years of marriage, I immediately became fearful of what would become of me. I was used to two incomes and was worried about how I would be able to maintain my lifestyle and manage the upkeep of my financial responsibilities. From 2012, until the day that I filed for divorce, I depended on my husband and his income to sustain us and provide for the family. I took the Bible's version of "Help Meet" seriously. My goal was to be the Proverbs 31 wife that supported her husband, took care of the household, and demonstrated the love of God towards all I came in contact with. When my husband's resources were low, I would "help meet" the needs of our family. We never lacked financially because "when one fell, the other was there to pick them up." However, when I filed for divorce, I did not realize how not having two incomes would impact me.

However, finances were only one area that affected me after the divorce. I was also impacted mentally, emotionally, physically, and spiritually. All of those areas affected me hard, and I had to find myself all over again. Because of the devastating circumstances, the divorce had to happen. It was non-negotiable. In marriages, there are some things that with effort, forgiveness, and love, the marriage can be restored, but there are other situations that can completely disintegrate a marriage. My marriage was disintegrated. However, I did not realize the magnitude of the aftermath that would emerge as a result of it.

After the divorce, I did not know how I was going to make it financially. I had been so dependent on my husband that I had not counted the cost of how things would be taken care of. All I knew was that I had to get out. This was when I learned to rely wholly on God for every aspect of my life. We err when we try to take care of everything in our own strength, but when we trust in God and His divine leading, we will avoid many pitfalls and heartaches. While we may feel reliant on others for income, companionship, or support, our ultimate provision comes from God. I was always able to depend on my husband for whatever I needed. If he didn't have it, he was going to make a way to get it. For that, I will always be thankful. However, in Matthew 6:33, Jesus instructs us to seek first the kingdom of God and His righteousness, and all these things will be added. This verse highlights the importance of prioritizing God's kingdom and trusting Him to provide for our needs. Our dependency should rest securely on God, recognizing His faithfulness and sufficiency in meeting all our needs.

I remember stressing so badly that I found myself in a panic attack. My heart was racing, and my anxiety was through the roof. Tears were flowing down my cheeks uncontrollably. It was at that moment that the Holy Spirit reminded me that He alone was my source in every aspect and area of my life. This realization caused me to refocus on the source, which is God, and to trust Him with everything within me. God knows what we have need of even before we ask, and it gives Him great pleasure to meet our needs. We must solely lean on and depend on Him. In doing so, we show those around us what peace and consolation it brings to trust in a God who can and will provide for you.

From that moment to this day, God has provided for me and continues to provide everything I need, want, and desire. I often tell people that I can't think of one thing in my life that I have ever needed that God did not provide. He's just that kind of Father. Faithful and dependable. When you find yourself stressing about how you are going to make it, just remember who the Source of all your needs is. Relinquish your needs to God by faith and watch how He will provide for you. All you have to do is trust Him.

Lessons Learned

- My goal was to be the Proverbs 31 wife that supported her husband, took care of the household, and demonstrated the love of God.

- In marriages, there are some things that with effort, forgiveness and love, the marriage can be restored, but there are other situations that completely disintegrates a marriage.

∽ We err when we try to take care of everything in our own strength, but when we trust in God and His divine leading, we will avoid many pitfalls and heartaches.

∽ When you find yourself stressing about how you are going to make it, just remember who the Source of all your needs is.

My Thoughts

Lesson 2

Don't' Allow "The People" to People

"Brethren, if a man be overtaken in a fault, ye which are spiritual, restore such a one in the spirit of meekness; considering thyself, lest thou also be tempted. Bear ye one another's burdens, and so fulfil the law of Christ."
~Galatians 6:1-2

My husband and I were married about six years when he told me that God had called him to start his own church, so we started a ministry from our home and invited people over. I did everything I could to support and stand behind my husband's calling. We constantly prayed together for direction, and eventually moved into a building. I helped him build the church from the ground up. God sent members to our church, and we were doing the work of the Lord. However, when it was made clear that we would be divorcing, we had to inform the church right away because we lived in Arkansas at the time, and they put your name in the newspaper if you got a divorce; so we needed to tell the church first before it hit the papers. When the time came, we stood before the congregation together and told them the news. That was my last time attending that church.

That day was the beginning of the gossip and hurtful things that would be said about me. Not only did I have to deal with the situation that led to my divorce, but I also had to deal with the gossip, the whispers, the lies, and the betrayal of people. I was grappling with feelings of shock, disbelief, and deep hurt, questioning not only with the authenticity of my marriage, but also the relationships and friendship that I thought I had. While married to the pastor, I was adored and respected by the congregation, playing a significant role within the church community. However, once the divorce was made public, the shift in how people treated me was immediate and swift. People began to gossip, often blaming me for the breakup without knowing the story or complexities of what had happened. It felt as though the same people who once offered smiles and support were now speaking ill of me behind my back. This judgment and rejection from a community I had served and loved were deeply painful. Despite this, I learned the importance of maintaining my dignity and composure. Walking with my head held high and choosing not to engage in gossip or justify my personal decisions to others were crucial for maintaining my self-respect. The experience taught me to rely on my faith and inner strength during such a devastating time.

For some odd reason, we have this part of us that is inclined to believe that people's opinions of us matter; so much so, that we do things to "people please" and in return we end up hurt, damaged and wounded. During the turbulent time following my divorce, my faith was what helped me navigate the emotional storms that came. Prayer became a daily refuge where I could lay my burdens before God and seek peace in the middle of all the chaos. Reading the Bible provided me with strength and guidance reminding me of God's promises and His presence in my life, especially during moments when I felt alone and misunderstood.

The challenge of dealing with gossip was compounded when people attempted to involve me in messy conversations about my ex-husband. It was painful to hear rumors and critical comments from those who were trying to stir up trouble rather than offer support. In those moments, I had to be firm yet respectful, letting people know that I would not entertain gossip about my ex-husband. I made it clear that such conversations were neither helpful nor welcome. Shutting down those conversations was about protecting my own peace. By redirecting the focus to positive, supportive interactions, I reinforced my commitment to living a life aligned with my faith, where grace, forgiveness, and love outweighed the hurt and bitterness that could have easily taken root in my heart.

From the outside looking in, people will always have opinions about what others should do in their lives. They are always going to talk. Let them! I have since learned that you cannot control what people think about you, what they say about you or their opinions of you. You will never be able to control people because people are human, and they will be people. I was so worried about what people were saying, that at one point, my decisions were based on how things "looked" to the public. Image was my priority. But regardless of how much I tried to keep things at bay, to keep down the gossip as much as possible, they still talked. Each whisper, phone call, text message or rumor that I heard, hurt me deeply, because they came from people in the church, those that I had prayed for and labored with during their distresses and tribulations. These were people who I had allowed to get close to me.

I had shared my vulnerabilities with some of them and they turned around and used that information against me. Many ugly things were said as I was going through that rough season of divorce in my life. It was even said that I wasn't saved because I was divorcing my husband since God hates divorce. I believe the Word, so I do believe that God hates divorce, but I also know that God's grace is sufficient, and His mercy endures forever. God knows the situation surrounding my divorce and He understands and has forgiven me. Hearing all the gossip that was getting back to me was hurtful, disappointing, and discouraging to the extent that I felt like physically fighting, cursing some out and exposing others. Some went through great lengths to tell lies about my situation and it was unbelievable to me.

As of this writing, it has been two years and I have since learned valuable lessons about people. As long as they "think" that you are in a coveted position and doing well, they will uplift you, encourage you, compliment you and honor you, but the minute something in your life goes wrong, that all changes. The true nature of people will be revealed. These are people who should have been and should be PRAYing instead of PREYing.

During that rough season in my life after my divorce, I cried out to God and asked Him if He was angry with me for divorcing. I also asked Him if I still had a chance to be what He had created and called me to be. His response to me was, *"I See. I Know. I understand."* Not only that, but He also let me know that He hadn't changed his mind concerning me. Most times, people forget about the grace that they themselves needed at one time of their life or another and was made available to them in their time of need, but when it comes to others, they don't deserve the same grace that God made available to them. God said to me, *"Don't allow guilt and shame to guilt and shame you back into something that I have already delivered you from."* It's important that we only focus on God's view of us because that is the only view that matters. When battling between the opinion of people and God's view of us, I encourage you to choose God every time because people will be people, but God never changes.

Lessons Learned

- From the outside looking in, people will always have opinions about what others should do in their lives. People are always going to talk. Let them!

- During the turbulent time following my divorce, my faith was what helped me navigate the emotional storms that came.

- I have since learned that you cannot control what people think about you, what they say about you or their opinions of you.

My Thoughts

<h1 style="text-align:center">Lesson 3</h1>

Every Fight isn't your Fight

*"For the Lord your God is the one who goes with you to
fight for you against your enemies to give you victory."*
Deuteronomy 20:4

I'll never forget my first fight in middle school. It is still etched in my memory. There was this girl who bullied me relentlessly while in school and I went home crying about it every day. On one particular day when I came home crying because of her, my grandfather told me that, that day would be the last time that I would come home crying. He told me that the next day when I went to school, I was going to finally fight her, and win! My response to him was, "But I don't know how to fight." Determined to put an end to it, he said, "I'm going to teach you." He took me outside behind the garage and taught me a winning technique that guaranteed my victory over my bully. He told me to punch her in the face, then immediately twist my fist when I do it. When we finished, his words to me were simple but firm: "And you better win!"

The next day, I went to school filled with so much courage. I approached her and said, *"You have been picking on me every day and today, we're gonna fight."* She was bent over her locker when I confronted her and when she stood up, I did just what my grandfather taught me. Yes, I hit her first! She began bleeding from the side of her face her jaw area. After I hit her, I said, *"And whenever I see you, you better go the other way!"* After that, whenever she saw me, she would turn around and go the other way, just like I told her to do. From that day forward, I was not afraid of anyone or anything. As I grew older, I carried my grandfather's lessons with me in every aspect of my life. To this day, I have a winner's mentality and I cannot stand to lose. If ever I do lose, it is not because I did not fight.

As far as my bully, I never had a problem out of her again. However, I saw her in Walmart years later. We were both big and grown, but when she saw me in Walmart, she went in the opposite direction. I went up to her and apologized for what had happened when we were children. She also apologized for bullying me. She was a mother and we stood in Walmart and talked about the effects that bullying has on children. We talked over two hours in the store and prior to going our separate ways, we hugged. However, when I became rooted in Christ, I learned that every battle is not meant for me to fight. For some battles, I can simply say, *"Lord, I am giving this to you.*" As men and women of God, we must learn to trust God. Every fight is not for us. Some situations happen for us to be able to see the salvation of the Lord in the land of the living. Although a fight may come to you, that does not mean that you have to fight back on your own. You can give it to God and watch how things work out. When we try to fight battles in our own strength - especially those that are too big for us, we end up overwhelmed, frustrated, and discouraged; but if we give it to God, we won't have to worry about going through any of that. When you go through difficult times, it's easy to run to a corner, cower down and hide, hoping that when you tiptoe out, the situation will be gone or people will have forgotten about it, but the truth is that the situation is still there, and people do not forget very easily. The situation will not change, and until you decide what you are going to do, it will remain there. Doing nothing, is not an option.

During the most vulnerable moments of my divorce, I felt attacked. There was one incident that hurt me to the core. I received a phone call from a member of my church. When I answered, she seemed to be very upset and kept repeating, *"the picture, the picture!"* I asked her to calm down and tell me what she was trying to say. Once she collected herself, she said, *"The picture that was in the foyer of the church. The one of you and the pastor has been taken down."* She then said, *"That picture represented hope for me, and now it's gone and replaced with a picture of just him."* To hear that they had taken my picture down, hurt me deeply. I was not only hurt, but angry as well. Although I was officially divorced, I felt that it was too soon to take my picture down. At the time of the call, I was in the airport and began pacing back and forth. I thought to myself, *"How could he?"* We hadn't even been divorced thirty days. The ink had not dried on the papers yet and my picture was already taken down. I had helped build that church and my picture came down as though I had never existed and none of my sacrifices had mattered. There were so many thoughts running through my mind at that moment. After learning about the picture, I wanted to do something just as hurtful to him so that he could feel the hurt that I was feeling at that moment. I did not know what to do with the influx of emotions that were overtaking me.

That season of my life was very difficult. Going places and running into people who knew about the divorce was awkward and uncomfortable for me, which was why all I wanted to do was stay in the house. I would hear of the chatter when I would go different places and I could feel the stares and whispers. The blame for the divorce was being placed on me although no one knew the real reason for the divorce other than me, him and the Lord. I wanted so badly to stand on the rooftop and tell everything. I wanted to tell my side of the story, but the Lord had me to keep silent and let Him handle it. That was one of the hardest things I had ever had to do, but I knew what the Lord had told me to do - and that was to keep quiet. I knew that in time, all would be revealed, but it had to be in God's timing. It was so hard not telling the world my truth, but I did it. I asked God for the strength to pray for those who were gossiping about me, and I prayed for strength to make it through each day with grace and dignity.

I had witnessed firsthand how ugly, nasty, and acrimonious divorces could be because I had seen the effects of it among many people that I knew, and some within ministry. I had watched people leave churches hurt and bruised over, never to return as a result of what they were going through. As the first lady of the church, my prayer from the very beginning was, *"Lord don't allow anyone to stumble because of my decisions."* By virtue of my position as the pastor's wife, I knew that eyes would always be on me, and I never wanted anyone to be discouraged or lose their faith in our Lord because of me. That's why I didn't fight in the natural. I knew that the situation was bigger than me. The way that I handled myself before, during and after my divorce would affect others in some way. I needed to be a woman of wisdom who handled the situation with class and grace. Anything less than that would not bespeak that of a Christian woman of God. Lives and souls were on the line, and I did not want anyone's blood to be on my hands. People were watching me to see how I would react.

I learned so much about people during that time. They will love you when they perceive that your life is ideal, but the minute you begin to publicly experience life's trials and tests, they will turn on you like yesterday's trash because you no longer fit into that box that they had placed you into within their minds. There were those who tried to ruin my reputation because I chose the quiet route, and they used my silence as a weapon against me. However, I refused to allow them to get me to step out of my character. Reputation is who people say that you are. Character is who you really are and present yourself as, so my character was on display daily, and I was strategic about my moves and words.

Every time I made the decision not to run and hide, I was pushing through spiritually. It hurt, but I kept showing up and I kept smiling. God was building me, guiding me, teaching me and making me better. In the book of Psalms 34:19, it declares that, *"Many are the afflictions of the righteous but the Lord will deliver them out of them all."* That Word is true, and He did deliver me. It is so very important that when trials and challenges come into your life, you are mindful of how you move. Every fight isn't your fight. Go forward knowing that God's grace is sufficient for you. Whatever you do, Keep showing up.

I love God and I trust Him, but when you say you trust God, there will come a time when you have to prove it. You will be tested in every area that you say you believe in to see if what you say it truly what you believe. You cannot just speak it. You will be tested in it. From a Christian woman's perspective, facing a situation as emotionally charged as divorce, requires an understanding that not every battle is ours to fight. Scripture reminds us to, "Be still, and know that I am God." (Psalm 46:10). This is a powerful verse for those times when our instinct is to take matters into our own hands. In these moments, relinquishing control and allowing God to lead is not a sign of weakness but one of great faith.

In the throes of divorce, the urge to counter accusations, engage in the gossip, or defend my own honor was overwhelming. However, this time of my life was a pivotal opportunity to practice the humility that Christ modeled. By stepping back, I allowed God to work in my life in ways I could not do on my own. He fought for me in unseen ways, turning what could have been my reactive battles into testimonies of His grace. Choosing to respond with silence and dignity to the hurtful gossip and blame was not about me being passive. It was about being anchored in God's promises. It was about knowing that my identity and worth are rooted in Him, not in the opinions of others. This quiet strength was not merely about outward appearances but was a deep, spiritual practice of trust and surrender.

Moreover, maintaining my silence and moving forward with grace under pressure cultivated a strength of character in me that elevated me spiritually. It allowed me to reflect Christ's character, who, even in His most challenging moments, responded with love and patience. As we strive to emulate Him, we mature, our faith deepens, and we find peace in the assurance that God is in control, shaping our path for His glory and our good. Just always keep in mind that every fight is not your fight.

Lessons Learned

- To this day, I have a winner's mentality and I cannot stand to lose.

- I carried my grandfather's lesson with me in every aspect of my life. To this day, I have a winner's mentality and I cannot stand to lose. If ever I do lose, it is not because I did not fight.

- Choosing to respond with silence and dignity to the hurtful gossip and blame was not about me being passive. It was about being anchored in God's promises.

My Thoughts

Lesson 4

You'll Feel Lonely, but you are Not Alone

"And lo, I am with you always, even unto the end of the world." ~Matthew 28:20

I can't even begin to put into words how lonely I felt going through the divorce process. The end of my marriage triggered profound sadness, feelings of loneliness and loss of interest in leaving the house. I temporarily struggled to find meaning in my life and experienced a bit of despair. This life change was not something I had anticipated or even saw coming. I had been blindsided by everything that had led up to the divorce. The societal judgments and stigma surrounding me and my divorce only compounded things, undermining my sense of self-worth. Although I was surrounded by friends and family, I still felt lonely. There was the feeling of a great loss, which left an empty void. A few days after my divorce was finalized, some of my then closest friends came over to support me to ensure that I was okay. We just sat there in silence. I began to cry and asked, *"What am I going to do now?"* One of my friends then asked me this question: *"What does Venisha like to do?"* I honestly couldn't answer because for the past ten years I had spent my life supporting and doing what brought joy and pleasure to my husband. I had totally forgotten about myself and what I wanted to do, the things that brought me joy. I had become accustomed to doing ministry, and even though it was sometimes burdensome, I knew that it was what he enjoyed, so I wanted to be a part of what brought pleasure to him. I had given so much of myself to supporting my husband in the ministry that I neglected doing some of the things that brought me joy.

One day, I felt so alone and so lonely. I had a great desire to talk to someone, so I called a friend, but she wasn't not available. I then called another friend, but talking to her made me feel even worse than I did before I called her. She too had been through a divorce, and it was obvious that she was bitter and was still harboring some negative feelings about it. Needless-to-say, she did not help me feel better about my situation. Many people go through divorce and although the final decision to dissolve the marriage is never good, all divorces are not the same. Some are amicable while others are acrimonious. Everyone experiences divorce in different ways, but there is always the element of sadness and loss that is felt. There is also a feeling of failure, hurt, in some cases, depression or shame and a general sense of rejection.

These emotions, if not properly dealt with can turn into emotional baggage. When this baggage has not been appropriately dealt with, it seeps out little by little and sabotages new relationships that would otherwise have long-term potential. When we hear the term emotional baggage, we automatically think of women, but men carry emotional baggage as well. They experience the same emotions that women do, but since it is not socially acceptable for men to carry their emotions on their shoulders, they do a good job of hiding what they are feeling. However, they too want to stay in their beds under the covers when they are going through something as devastating as a divorce or even a broken heart. Baggage comprises all of those emotions. Life's experiences change us for better or for worse.

Those who go through it need a strong support system. They need others to lift them up and encourage them as they heal. Unfortunately, there are some cases where people who have gotten a divorce, seem to forget what it took for them to overcome the hurt, sadness and feelings of rejections resulting from the process and are unsympathetic to others who are now walking the same road they walked. Those are the ones who make you feel worse when speaking with them about your own situation. I learned the hard way. It is therefore very important to have discernment, even in difficult times. The Holy Spirit will lead you to the right person to talk to or He will even send that person to you.

I was deeply frustrated during that time, but God spoke to me and comforted me. That day when that I tried reaching out to people for comfort is the day that I learned that everyone isn't assigned to help me sort through my issues. I had to lean on God for that. That is what He was teaching me. We must trust and hold on to the word in difficult times. These are the exact times that your faith is tried and when the Word is tried. During these times, we must read and resonate on comforting scriptures such as the ones below:

- **Psalm 34:17-18:** "The righteous cry, and the Lord heareth, and delivers them out of all their troubles. The Lord is nigh unto them that are of a broken heart; and saves such as be of a contrite spirit."

- **Romans 8:28:** "And we know that all things work together for good to them that love God, to them who are the called according to his purpose."

- **2 Corinthians 12:9:** "And he said unto me, My grace is sufficient for thee: for my strength is made perfect in weakness. Most gladly therefore will I rather glory in my infirmities, that the power of Christ may rest upon me."

- **Isaiah 41:10:** "Fear thou not; for I am with thee: be not dismayed; for I am thy God: I will strengthen thee; yea, I will help thee; yea, I will uphold thee with the right hand of my righteousness."

- **James 1:2-4:** "My brethren, count it all joy when ye fall into divers temptations; Knowing this, that the trying of your faith worketh patience. But let patience have her perfect work, that ye may be perfect and entire, wanting nothing."

- **1 Peter 5:7:** "Casting all your care upon him; for he cares for you."

- **Psalm 55:22:** "Cast thy burden upon the Lord, and he shall sustain thee: he shall never suffer the righteous to be moved."

- **Philippians 4:13:** "I can do all things through Christ which strengthens me."

- **Psalm 46:1-2:** "God is our refuge and strength, a very present help in trouble. Therefore, will not we fear, though the earth be removed, and though the mountains be carried into the midst of the sea;"

- **Romans 5:3-5:** "And not only so, but we glory in tribulations also: knowing that tribulation worketh patience; And patience, experience; and experience, hope: And hope maketh not ashamed; because the love of God is shed abroad in our hearts by the Holy Ghost which is given unto us."

These scriptures provided me with reassurance, strength, and a reminder of God's presence and provision during my difficult times.

When trust has been broken and your life has been turned upside down and shattered by challenges, it becomes hard to believe that things are going to get better. It is difficult to see your way out of your current situation because you are so clouded by the dark clouds, but just keep looking past that cloud and you will begin to see the SON. As you trust in God, day by day, things will get better and the new day will be better than the day before until you finally realize that you are no longer in that dark place. It can even be a challenge to believe that God is there and that He will bring you through, but He will. While you are in the fire, your perception is distorted and you don't see clearly, but regardless of how you may feel, if you belong to God, then He is right there. His angels are also right there comforting and strengthening you. I cried for hours that day. I felt so alone. I felt that everyone was living their beautiful lives, but that God had forgotten about me. Meanwhile, I was hurt, broken, sad, disappointed and alone, trying to reconcile a myriad of emotions that I was experiencing. The pieces were all over the floor and I had no idea where to even begin picking them up.

I desired the ear of those around me, but what I really needed was the ear of God. When I finally came to myself, I realized that the only constant in my life was God; and He had been there for me the whole time. There isn't anyone in the world who can have your back like God. He will not forsake you. He won't turn His back on you, and he won't gossip about you to others. He is the one who satisfies your deepest longings and gives you purpose and meaning in life. Even on those days when we feel alone, we are never alone. God is always there.

Lessons Learned

- Everyone experiences divorce in different ways, but there is always the element of sadness and loss that is felt.

- We must trust and hold on to the word in difficult times. These are the exact times that your faith is tried and when the Word is tried.

- The Holy Spirit will lead you to the right person to talk to or He will even send that person to you.

My Thoughts

<h1 style="text-align:center">Lesson 5</h1>

Keep Your Peace

"Thou wilt keep him in perfect peace, whose mind is stayed on thee, because he trusteth in thee" ~Isaiah 26:3

Inner peace is a state of calmness and contentment in a person's heart and mind, regardless of what is happening around them. This tranquility stems from the assurance of God's presence and promises, and not from external circumstances. Inner peace is a deep sense of harmony that comes from a deep relationship with God, and surpasses worldly circumstances. From a Christian perspective, peace is described as the "peace of God, which passes all understanding" (Philippians 4:7), implying that it is a type of peace that cannot be fully understood or replicated. This peace is a gift from God, given to those who live in accordance with His will and trust in His divine providence. Peace is a blessing, and we must protect it at all costs.

Many people who appear to have prosperous lives can still experience internal turmoil. This disconnect occurs because material achievements, popularity and worldly success are unstable and temporary. They depend on factors that can change or disappear suddenly; but the peace offered by God is eternal and unshakable, rooted in the eternal nature of God Himself. Inner peace affects every aspect of a person's life, including the ability to think clearly, make wise decisions, and interact with others in a loving and compassionate manner. Peace gives strength and stability in times of adversity, reduces stress and anxiety, and leads to a fuller, more meaningful existence. This peace enables us to live out our faith authentically and respond to life's challenges with grace and confidence, rather than fear and uncertainty.

I have learned that we must be vigilant because there are things that come to bring distraction or disturb our peace. If we are not watchful, we can get caught up in the enemy's attempt to get us off track. I remember a time that I was at Salt Grass Steakhouse celebrating the birthday of my sister's friend when my former husband called me. As soon as I said, *"Hello,"* I could immediately tell that he was perturbed about something, and his voice was visibly angry. He then said, *"I don't know what you have been telling people, but I don't have a problem with you."* I was confused as to what he was talking about because I had not discussed him with anyone to make them think that we had a problem with each other or with being in each other's presence; and that's what I told him. I later learned that he was upset because the friend that I was celebrating with that day, who was a mutual friend of both of us, had not invited him to the celebration because the friend didn't want me to feel uncomfortable. During the conversation, I became agitated to the extent that it changed my entire disposition.

Upon returning to the event where everyone was in the restaurant, they could all see that my entire disposition and countenance had changed, and they all began asking if I was I okay. It took me a minute to settle myself and when I did, I asked God what the lesson was in that. Later on, the answer dropped in my spirit. Prior to going to the event earlier that day, I had spent time in the presence of God. I was in a state of peace and joy after being in God's presence. The Word of God says in Psalm 16:11 that *"Thou wilt shew me the path of life: in thy presence is fulness of joy"* and I had definitely experienced His joy that day, but unbeknownst to me, the enemy strategically tried to steal that joy from me - and he succeeded. That was the lesson that I was to learn - to be watchful and not allow anyone to steal my joy.

Life will sometimes bring situations and circumstances that can disrupt our inner peace. Whether it's financial worries, relationship issues, health concerns, or job-related stress, these can fill our minds and rob us of the serenity that God intends for us. When our focus shifts towards our problems, rather than the peace that Christ offers, we can easily find ourselves overwhelmed and separated from God's calming presence. Jesus Himself addressed this issue when He said, "Peace I leave with you, my peace I give unto you: not as the world giveth, give I unto you. Let not your heart be troubled, neither let it be afraid" (John 14:27). This passage shows us the unique peace that comes from Christ, a peace that differs totally from what the world considers as peace because it doesn't depend on external circumstances.

Maintaining inner peace requires a conscious effort to stay rooted in Christ and in prayer. Prayer connects us to God and allows us to cast our cares on Him as He instructed us to do in 1 Peter 5:7 where it is written, "Casting all your care upon him; for he careth for you." Through prayer, we open our hearts to God and find strength in His omnipresence. Another scripture that speaks about peace is Philippians 4:7, which promises that "the peace of God, which passeth all understanding, shall keep your hearts and minds through Christ Jesus." This scripture serves as an anchor that prevents us from being swept away by life's storms. However, when we neglect prayer and the Word, and focus on all the negative that is happening around us, we fail to guard our peace and we leave ourselves vulnerable to the chaos of the world. Without God's peace, minor issues can escalate in our minds, leading to overwhelming stress and, potentially, a mental breakdown. Trials and tribulations are inevitable, and they come to everyone; but our responses to them can impact our mental and spiritual health. By prioritizing our relationship with God through prayer and scripture, we can navigate even the most trying times with a peace that not only endures but empowers us to face life's challenges with resilience and hope.

Allowing someone to disturb your inner peace is a sure-fire way to take you out of the presence of God. While with my friends in that restaurant, I had been laughing, socializing and having good time when the enemy tried to pull me out of that happy place through that one phone call. After hanging up from speaking with him, I had to make a conscious decision to hold on to my peace, refocus and enjoy my evening.

So many times in life, the enemy will use those closest to us to disturb our peace. We must realize that in moments of attacks and confusion, we do not wrestle against flesh and blood. We are not fighting physical beings, but the spirit of the enemy operating through them that is seeking to attack both parties. We cannot succumb to the tricks and schemes of the enemy. If we choose to stay in God's presence, not only will we experience the peace of God, but ultimately, we will experience joy. Remember to guard your peace.

Lessons Learned

- We must be vigilant against anything that comes to bring distraction or disturb our peace.

ﮧ Allowing someone to disturb your peace is a
sure-fire way to take you out of the presence
of God.

ﮧ Without God's peace, minor issues can
escalate in our minds, leading to
overwhelming stress and, potentially, a
mental breakdown.

My Thoughts

Lesson 6

Crying Is Actually Healing

"You keep track of all my sorrows. You have collected all my tears in your bottle, you have recorded each one in your book." ~Psalm 56:8

During that trying time of my life, I spent many days and nights crying what seemed to be uncontrollable, never-ending tears. I would try to stop, but they would just keep coming. I finally allowed myself to feel every emotion that came to me and let the tears flow. I asked God why I was crying so much, and it was then that He spoke to my spirit. Not only were my tears cleansing me, but they were also healing me. The tears that I cried were a release. All the hurt, the shame, the anger, every emotion that I felt was being released through my tears. It was a purging process that did not feel good, but it was good for me.

During this difficult time in my life, I learned so many lessons. One of the main things I learned was that life doesn't stop to cater to you because something traumatic has happened. You've got to keep pushing and keep moving forward no matter how hard it seems to do so. There were many days that I did not want to leave the house. I just wanted to stay home, cry, and wallow in my misery but life goes on and I had to get up, get dressed and go to work. At that juncture of my life, I needed to take care of myself and pay bills, so I had to go to work. I no longer had someone to rely on to contribute. It was all me now. God gave me the strength and courage to get myself together and keep moving forward despite how I was feeling. It was only by His grace that I did not look like what I was going through. I was able to talk to people, smile, laugh and socialize - although on the inside, I was broken, sad and deeply hurt. There were days that the reality of what had happened, would hit me. *"Girl you are divorced! You are really divorced!"*

The enemy would try to attack my mind and pull me into a depression, but he did not succeed. Although my anxiety was at an all-time high and I would have crying spells, God still kept me through it all. I would be sitting at my desk and would start crying out of nowhere. Those who saw me and knew what I was going through, were supportive and knew exactly what to say to me during those times. Even my supervisor at that time was understanding. When she perceived that the weight of my emotions was too much, she would say to me, *"Go home and try again tomorrow."* Not everyone would be that understanding and as I look back, I can clearly see that God surrounded me with people that understood my fragility during that time and extended their compassion. May He bless them for their kindness towards me.

Everyone knows what it feels to cry because everyone has experienced it. Crying is a natural response to various emotions that we go through in this life such as sadness, depression, frustration, hurt, disappointment, rejection, etc. If not properly expressed, these emotions often overwhelm us, but tears can also be a healthy expression way of letting things out. Crying can make us feel vulnerable and exposed, yet it also brings a sense of release. When we cry, we are not only expressing our emotions but also allowing ourselves to process and confront what we are feeling. We do not realize it at the time, but this can lead to emotional healing. Our tears can be a means through which God begins to heal our brokenness.

In the Bible, we see numerous instances where people cried out to God in their distresses, and God responded with comfort and healing. Crying can be seen as a form of cleansing as well. Tears can wash away emotional pain that clouds our hearts. In moments of sorrow and hurt, turning to God and allowing ourselves to cry while releasing our feelings to him can be a great act of faith. It shows our trust in Him to heal us acknowledging that He understands and cares about our suffering. Crying is not a sign of weakness, but it is a part of the human experience that God fully understands. The Bible reassures us that

God is close to the brokenhearted and saves those who are crushed in spirit (Psalm 34:18). He does not overlook our pain but sees each tear we shed. The Bible even speaks to how God collects our tears in a bottle when we cry. This act by God signifies that our tears are precious to Him, and He remembers each one. The scripture from the King James Version that reflects this is: *"Thou tellest my wanderings: put thou my tears into thy bottle: are they not in thy book?"* *(Psalm 56:8).*

This above verse reassures us that God is intimately aware of our suffering and keeps a record of our tears. It demonstrates His compassion and the love that He has for each of us. As we journey through life, different situations bring different emotions such as happiness, joy, sadness, anger, grief, frustration, discouragement, etc. We will also at some point experience a great test that can shake the very core of our faith. However, we can take comfort in knowing that God understands our pain and is always there to help us through it.

The other side of love and happiness is rejection. It can be the worst feeling in the world when the object of your love has broken your trust in the worst way. A feeling of rejection followed by feelings of embarrassment sets in and is sometimes replaced by sadness and depression. Betrayal can sometimes have the same feelings as rejection because in some strange way, the betrayal contains a level or rejection. Both betrayal and rejection are demeaning feelings that causes us to feel inferior and sometimes unworthy, but they too are phases of life that everyone should experience in order to learn and grow. Getting rejected teaches you to be strong as well as how to appropriately deal with others who you may have rejected so you can understand how they may have felt. We all want to have our love returned more than anything. Being betrayed or rejected does not always have to do with you and you should not allow your self-confidence to suffer because of it. What another person makes a conscience choice to do should not cause you to feel guilty in any way.

We are not to blame when someone has committed an offence against us. During my divorce process, one of the most important lessons I learned about betrayal is not to allow it to take root in me. At some point, I had to get up and say to myself that although he hurt me deeply, I cannot allow feelings of anger, bitterness, or resentment to take residence in me. I absolutely had to release and relinquish them to God. I was adamant that they were not going to hold me hostage and create a stronghold in my life. I loved my husband so much and I was committed to being his strong help meet, but I had to finally come to grips with the fact that getting divorced simply meant he was not meant for me. Point blank! There is no reason to remain upset with the person who you feel betrayed or rejected you. Do not put up a wall and not allow yourself to open up to a worthy person again and be loved in the future. You must move in the confidence and assurance that your hurt will be replaced by full and complete acceptance from someone else who will love you, be good to you and will not betray you.

We can find hope and encouragement when dealing with sadness and distress through prayer and reading God's Word. By reading the Bible and seeking God's guidance, we will find direction and hope in the midst of our pain. It is also therapeutic and cathartic to speak with trusted individuals about the things that have caused the sadness, discouragement or frustration. Everyone needs an outlet of expression and prayer is one of the best ways to heal, but so is crying. Give it to God and turn to Him in times of darkness, knowing that He is always there to guide you, lift you up, and bring you out. It is okay to cry. Tears are an act of cleansing, and there's absolutely nothing wrong with it. Rest assured that every tear represents your healing.

Lessons Learned:

- Life doesn't stop to cater to you because something traumatic has happened.

- God gave me the strength and courage to get myself together and keep moving forward despite how I was feeling.

❧ As I look back, I can clearly see that God surrounded me with people that understood my fragility during that time and extended their compassion.

❧ We can find hope and encouragement when dealing with sadness and distress through prayer and reading God's Word.

My Thoughts

It's Okay to set Boundaries

Be not deceived: evil communications corrupt good manners. ~1 Corinthians 15:33

Setting boundaries is very critical, especially for women trying to process the aftermath of a divorce from a marriage to a pastor. Boundaries serve as invisible yet powerful lines that define your personal space, values, and limits. Establishing these boundaries through your words, actions, and conversations is crucial in ensuring that others understand how to approach you. When you consistently demonstrate a track record of integrity, grace, and wisdom, you silently communicate your boundaries to those around you. Your behavior sets a standard, letting others know what is acceptable and what is not. For example, if you always handle situations with poise and assertiveness, people learn to respect your time and emotional space. Your consistent actions build a reputation that precedes you, making it clear how others should interact with you.

Setting boundaries helps you to maintain your dignity, respect, and emotional health. It ensures that others understand how to approach you and interact with you, based on the silent cues you provide through your consistent actions and behavior. Without boundaries, you risk being treated any kind of way and feeling overwhelmed and frustrated. With clear boundaries, you can protect yourself from uncomfortable situations, fostering a more positive and respectful environment for yourself. Boundaries are not just about keeping negative influences out, but they also protect your well-being and self-respect. When people see that you respect yourself enough to set and maintain boundaries, they are more likely to approach you with the same respect and consideration. This silent communication through consistent behavior ensures that your boundaries are recognized and respected, often without you needing to explain to people what they should and should not come to you with.

Never allow anything or anyone to cause you to deviate from the boundaries that you have established for yourself. The test comes when we are faced with temptations, which sometimes come unexpectedly. When we are faced with on-the-spot decisions, we must stand firm on our previously set boundaries. Boundaries protect you and stand as preventative maintenance to stop unhealthy situations before they start. God placed a moral compass in everyone. Therefore, doing what we know is wrong feels wrong from the start, but many override that feeling and eventually reach a point where their moral compass appears to no longer work. Boundaries are designed to be a dividing. Your moral compass is important and very much needed - especially in relationships.

Boundaries are the limits and rules that we set for ourselves within relationships and also friendships. They set the standard for how people can interact with you. When boundaries are not clear, you run the risk of being hurt. I had to set boundaries as I went through my process of divorce. I could not allow people who had been connected to both my former husband and me to come to me with information about him or what he may or may not have said or done. In doing so, I protected my peace and the possibly of encountering more hurt by being wounded more deeply than I already had been. I had to also be mindful of my reactions and responses when they were able to slip some information through.

Your actions and reactions are always being scrutinized and I had to be mindful of that at all times. People sometimes have the tendency to want to share gossip with you; and the motives are not always to be messy. It could just be because they think you care and want to know. Other times, they bring information because they *are* being messy and want to see if they can get a reaction out of you. That's where self-control comes into play and where I draw the line and let my boundaries be known. I made it clear that I was not interested in knowing anything about what my ex was doing or saying and that I would appreciate it if they did not come to me with information about him.

When it comes to boundaries, we must be careful that we do not cross them. After my divorce, my ex-husband had his first Pastor's anniversary without me. A statement that he made was brought back to me. Apparently, he said, *"Thank God for Venisha and all she did."* The statement apparently was meant to be negative, implying that had I not done what I did by divorcing him, he would not be where he was, suggesting that he was in a better place. Since the divorce was fresh and I was still trying to heal and get over all that had happened, things were raw, so the message really bothered me. The statement made about me in front of the congregation hurt me to my core and felt like salt was just poured on a wound. I felt that he did not and should not have mentioned me at all. Afterwards, he and I had a heated conversation about it, and I made it known that I was upset and hurt about the statement; but he said something to me that made me really think. He said, *"Venisha, here's the reality: we are divorced."* That's when another lesson came to me.

I learned that although he did not have to say anything at all about me because we were no longer married, what he said should not have been my

56

concern. I also learned that I must be mindful of the motives people have when approaching me with information about my ex-husband. Although they may have known us both, I still did not need them approaching me with anything pertaining to my ex and that he was an ex for a reason. The main lesson learned was that I did not need to know about anything what was happening in his life or in the church. That was a boundary that I did not need anyone to cross. All of that was my past and I no longer needed to be concerned about it anymore. I was no longer there and needed to look forward to my future. Although the boundaries can be hard because I too had to follow them, they saved me from future days of hurt and tears. Having set boundaries has allowed me to heal since I do not allow negativity to cross the line of divide. No matter how much you may want to know, you don't need to know everything. Mind your own business, focus on your future and save yourself the heartache and pain of it all. Never allow anyone to cross the boundaries of divide that you have set.

Failing to establish boundaries can lead to many challenges. Without clear boundaries, people may feel entitled to encroach upon your personal space, time, and emotional well-being. They may think nothing about approaching you with gossip, their expectations of you, or behaviors that are disrespectful or inappropriate. The absence of boundaries can lead to feelings of being overwhelmed, taken advantage of, or emotionally drained. When others think that you do not have set limits, they may treat you in any way they choose, often without consideration for your feelings or needs. This can result in uncomfortable situations, strained relationships, and a diminished sense of self-worth. You may find yourself constantly reacting to the demands and expectations of others, rather than living according to your own values and priorities.

Lessons Learned:

- When you consistently demonstrate a track record of integrity, grace, and wisdom, you silently communicate your boundaries to those around you.

- Your actions and reactions are always being scrutinized and I had to be mindful of that at all times.

- Although the boundaries can be hard because I too had to follow them too, they saved me from future days of hurt and tears.

My Thoughts

<h1 style="text-align:center">Lesson 8</h1>

Forgiveness Is Divine

"And be ye kind one to another, tenderhearted, forgiving one another, even as God for Christ's sake hath forgiven you" ~Ephesians 4:32

Forgiveness is a key component in our relationship with God and with others. When we forgive, we are releasing the grip of anger, hurt, shame, and bitterness from our hearts and choosing to extend grace to those who have wronged us. No matter how bad the hurt or disloyalty was, we must find the strength to let go and choose to extend forgiveness in the same way that God has forgiven us. Holding on to grudges and resentment will only weigh you down and prevent you from living a life of peace and joy.

Unforgiveness is the greatest block to healing. Without forgiving, total healing is impossible. Forgiveness is the foundation that starts the healing process. The inability to forgive has been the greatest roadblock that blocks a deliverance from occurring. Unforgiveness is one of the primary tools that Satan uses to gain a stronghold into the life of a Christian.

He is very strategic. He works somewhat like this: You love the Lord. Your life is predicated on praise, worship, fasting and loving your sisters and brothers in Christ. Satan has to stop your effectiveness because you are advancing the kingdom of God too much. He enters into a person close to you and uses them to hurt you deeply. The seed of hurt, disappointment and anger has now been planted in you. The offense they did to you was too much to forgive, so you hold on to the bitterness, disappointment, and unforgiveness. Now it becomes a part of you. Your prayers are now hindered. You are no longer as effective in the spirit as you once were, but you are trying to move forward in the same way you were prior to the hurt, but you can't because unforgiveness has taken root in you and until you deal with the issue and sincerely forgive, you will never be as effective in the spirit as you once were.

Unforgiveness can actually cause disease. It is a very powerful emotion, if not the most powerful emotion next to love. Spiritually, it keeps you in bondage. unforgiveness is a stronghold, having a very "strong" "hold" on a person. One is never truly free, nor can they walk in total liberty as long as they are holding unforgiveness in their heart toward anybody. I learned that forgiveness is one-sided. You do not need the other person in order to forgive them. You simply release what they did to you from your consciousness. When you think about what they did and it has no painful effect on you anymore, then you know you have released it. Forgiveness is simply a *decision* made by you to let it go and not to allow it to have a hold on you anymore. It is as easy as that. Forgiveness is not as hard as the devil makes it seem. I knew that I had to forgive my husband if I wanted to be free.

After my divorce was final, I found myself in a downward spiral. I knew I wasn't myself and ultimately, I felt like I was spinning out of control. I was an emotional wreck. However, I had been praying, but I knew that I needed something more. That's when I adopted the idea that therapy and prayer go hand in hand, so I began going to therapy twice a week for an hour. On my very first session, I noticed that the therapist had different seating arrangements set up. He told me that I could sit anywhere I wanted. There was a bean bag chair in a corner, so I plopped down on that and made myself comfortable. He introduced himself to me, and then asked, *"What brings you in today?"* I immediately began to cry uncontrollably. I cried big hard tears behind which were my hurt, shame and guilt. My tears also had sound as they fell. They told my story and how I had been feeling. The things that I had been holding inside bottled up were in every tear that fell from my eyes. I cried for an entire hour. The timer went off and my therapist asked, *"How do you feel now?"* I responded… *"Better."* He said *"Okay, well I will see you again Thursday same time."* I walked out of that office feeling like I had lost about thirty pounds. I knew however, that I was full, and I needed to go back to shed more.

I realized that I wasn't just shedding tears, but I was shedding everything that was behind those tears. When I returned, the therapist asked me the same question. *"What brings you in today?"* This time I was able to express without crying. I told him that I was recently divorced and that I felt like my life was out of control. I shared the details surrounding the divorce. He didn't say a word. He just listened and let me talk. Then I said, *"I just want to be able to forgive him and move on with my life."* It was at that time that the therapist spoke. He said, *"What will that change?"* I said, *"Well I'm a believer and I must forgive in order to be forgiven, and the quicker I forgive him, then the quicker I can go on with my life."* The therapist said, *"WOW! That's very admirable of you. I'm a believer as well; however, I think that you are too hard on yourself."* The next thing he said, clipped my wings and freed me. He said to me, *"Forgiveness is Divine."* He talked to me about how the human mind processes trauma. He said that if it's not properly filtered, then every time you experience something similar to what happened before, it would wound you again. He told me that forgiveness comes as you begin to filter. Sometimes it takes a little longer for people to do this, especially when they have been hit in the same area over and over.

During my therapy sessions, I realized that I did not do everything right in my marriage. I did not always say the right things or act in the right ways all the time. I had a part to play as well, and I was woman enough to admit those things. Because I needed my former husband's forgiveness, I in turn had to grant him the same. It's so easy to play the blame game. It's easy to weigh the offense, but it's not right and it's not mature. Although I didn't do anything close to what he did, there was still a breach somewhere. I am so thankful for therapy and prayer because they both allowed me an outlet of expression and taught me to understand things in perspective. Forgiveness is divine and it will come the moment you recognize your part in a situation or circumstance and begin to properly filter.

Lessons Learned:

- Forgiveness is the foundation that starts the healing process.

- No matter how bad the hurt or disloyal was, we must find the strength to let go and choose to extend forgiveness in the same way that God has forgiven us.

- Forgiveness comes as you begin to filter. Sometimes it takes a little longer for people to filter, especially when they have been hit in the same area over and over.

My Thoughts

<h1 style="text-align:center">Lesson 9</h1>

Don't Lose Focus

"Brethren, I count not myself to have apprehended: but thus one thing I do, forgetting those things which are behind, and reaching forth unto those things which are before, I press toward the mark for the prize of the high calling of God In Christ Jesus." ~ Philippians 3:13-14

In the journey of life, staying focused on what God has promised us in His Word is essential. His promises provide us with hope and assurance while guiding us through every season of change. We must also remain dedicated to our personal goals and aspirations, even in the midst of dark days, hurts, and times of testing. By keeping our eyes fixed on both God's promises we can navigate through life with purpose and direction. If we are not careful, we can easily lose focus. Our problems, tests, and trials can distract us, pulling our attention away from our goals and God's vision for our lives as outlined in His Word. When we divert our energy away from what the Word says and focus it on what we are going through, why this happened, what am I going to do, instead of maintaining our focus, we risk getting off track and eventually becoming derailed. This loss of focus can cause major delays in our achievements and hinder spiritual growth. If we allow ourselves to be consumed by the difficulties we face, we may cause delays in achieving our long-term goals. Similarly, when we forget God's promises during tough times, our faith can waver, slowing down spiritual progress. Losing focus leads to missed opportunities, extended periods of struggle, and a prolonged journey toward our desired outcomes.

On the other hand, staying focused expedites healing, opens doors, and keeps us aligned with the path that God has set before us. When we remain focused, our efforts are more directed and efficient, leading to quicker healing. Maintaining focus on God's promises strengthens our faith and enables us to overcome challenges with a sense of peace and confidence. Staying focused ensures we do not deviate from the path of blessings, forgiveness, and healing that God has laid out for us. By keeping our eyes on our goals and God's Word, we remain resilient and prepared to face any obstacles that come our way. Remember God's promises and keep your goals in sight. Despite the challenges you may face, trust in His Word, and continue working towards your aspirations. Staying focused will lead you to greater achievements, spiritual growth, and a life filled with God's blessings.

The enemy of your faith loves to constantly remind you of the hurts, betrayals, wounds, sins, and offences that you experienced and/or endured in the past, but dwelling on that negativity brings nothing good. Instead, you must redirect that thought energy towards the future that God has planned for you. You cannot afford to lose your focus on where God is taking you. Distractions will always come, but you must recognize them for what they are - distractions. Distractions are designed to cause you to lose focus and miss what God is doing in your life. The enemy will try and remind you of how a person betrayed you, hurt you, lied on you, acted towards you, or the horrible things they said to you or about you. You must be stronger than that though.

You must recognize negative thoughts when they come to you and have the mental strength to dismiss them and focus on things that are positive and make for peace. Forget about all the past hurts and release them. Just let them go as we talked about in the last chapter. I know that letting some things go can be hard, but with you and God working on it together, you can do it! Cast those negative elements on the Lord knowing that He cares for you according to 1 Peter 5:7. It is not easy, but if you really want to, you can do it. I had to learn to do this. I had to dismiss negative thoughts when they came to me - and there were so many. I had to forgive in order to heal, and I am still forgiving daily. As a result of me focusing on my future and forgiving, God has done things for me far greater than what I could have even imagined. I cannot afford to trip over the trivial. I must continue to learn, grow and find the lesson in everything. Everyone has their opinions and so many people wanted to give me theirs. They had advice on what they felt I should do and how I should do it. They said things like, *"If it was me, this is what I would do."* or, *"I would have handled that like this…"* I had to make a conscious decision to listen to God and not people. I would have created a big mess had I listened to people. The Bible tells us that there are many voices in the world, but I soon came to realize that the only voice I needed to hearken to, was the voice of God.

When I got ready to relocate, I called my former husband to ask him if he wanted anything out of the house before I sold it. He told me what he wanted, then let me know that he would be coming by to get them. The night before, I called him to confirm that he was coming. During the call, we began talking, and he told me how he felt about the way things had transpired during and after the divorce process. I felt as though I was being attacked, but I allowed him to speak, and I didn't interrupt him nor say a word. When he finally finished speaking, I asked him if he was done. When he said, *"Yes."* I said, *"Have a good night."* And I got off the phone. For some reason, I couldn't sleep that night. I tossed and turned.

The next day while praying, God spoke to me and said to call him back and let him know that I had heard him and apologize to him. I tried to reason with God and told Him that I had not done anything wrong.

It was my pride that did not want to do what God was directing me to do. I felt as though I didn't owe him an apology. I called some friends and told them what God had instructed me to do. They told me that if it was them, they would not apologize, but my response was, *"I am in a season where I need so much from God, so I cannot afford not to obey."* After speaking with them, God spoke to me again and said, *"Just like I am concerned about you, I am concerned about him."* I began to weep. I immediately picked up the phone and called him, but he didn't answer. I then said to myself, *"Well, this must not be you, God."* But then the phone rang immediately afterwards, and it was my ex-husband. I told him that when we last spoke, I had heard everything he said. I then apologized for the things he had mentioned that made him feel the way he did during our divorce process.

After that, I went on about my day. I had been obedient to what God had told me to do and I felt good about that. In the meantime, I had an unexpected bill to come up that needed to be taken care of immediately, but I didn't have the funds to pay it. I did not know what I was going to do. When my ex came to pick up the items he wanted from the house, he brought one of the members of the church with him. While in the house, he saw some pots and pans in a box in the kitchen and asked how much I wanted for them. I said, *"Just give me twenty dollars."* He took the pots and walked out. I went to the door and said,

"Hey you forgot to pay me." …so he reached into his pocket and pulled out two ten-dollar bills. He brought the money to me and then thanked me for all I had done for him and his mother while I was at the church. Then he walked away. He immediately turned back around while reaching into his right pocket and pulled out some money. Then he said, *"First Lady, wait. God told me to give you all the money in my pocket."* I began to cry crocodile tears. He hugged me and left. The money he gave me was enough to cover the bill that had come up with some funds left over. Had I not obeyed the voice of God, I don't believe that I would have been blessed in that way. I realized that when God instructs us to do something, it is because He has something in store that He is trying to do for you, but if we are not obedient, we will not be able to receive it, nor will we ever know what God had it mind for us. I know it gets hard, but I encourage you to press on regardless of what you go through. Don't allow the rough days to overwhelm you, and whatever you do, be obedient to God and don't lose your focus.

Lessons Learned:

- This loss of focus can cause major delays in our achievements and hinder spiritual growth. If we allow ourselves to be consumed by the difficulties we face, we may cause delays in achieving our long-term goals.

- You must recognize negative thoughts when
  they come to you and have the mental
  strength to dismiss them and focus on things
  that are positive and make for peace.

- As a result of me focusing on my future and
  forgiving, God has done things for me far
  greater than what I could have even imagined.

My Thoughts

Lesson 10

God is Fair

The Lord is righteous in all his ways, and holy in all his works. ~Psalm 145: 17

There are times in life when you have to grieve the loss of your expectations falling apart and still have the courage to look towards the future and believe again. Going through a divorce has continued to be a learning process for me. I think about the times when I felt as though I couldn't go on. I think about those times when I was no longer wanting to live. I had contemplated taking my own life and wanted nothing more than to just die. I just wanted to end the pain. I was numb to life. As I look back now, I can relate to the Psalmist in Psalm 27: 13-114 that says, *"What would have become of me, had I not believed that I would see the Lord's goodness in the land of the living!"* It was indeed good for me that I was afflicted, so that I might learn God's decrees (Psalm 119:71). Divorce is hard; having to endure the loss of something or someone valuable to you, is hard; grieving is hard as well, but if we allow God to guide us while we are in our wilderness experience, He will indeed bring us out. When we give it to Him, we see how it all worked out for our good. When we come out, we can look back and see that the Lord was with us the whole time. He was right there. God, in His infinite wisdom, has given us the precious gift of free will. This gift allows us the freedom to make our own decisions. However, when we make decisions without consulting God first, we often find that the outcomes are less than favorable. The result of not seeking God's guidance can be disappointing, sad, and frustrating, leading to feelings of regret, shame, hurt, or anger. When we face the consequences of our decisions, it is natural to feel upset and blame God, as though He led us into those difficult situations. Yet, if we take a step back and study God's characteristics and the way He moves, we will discover that the problems and disappointments we encounter are often the result of our own choices, not God's will for us.

God desires the best for us, and His ways are just and fair, but we tie His hands when we do not let Him guide us by asking Him to do so. God's fairness is very clear throughout the Bible. He is a God of justice, mercy, and unwavering faithfulness. Even when we make mistakes and fail to seek His guidance, He remains fair and just, always ready to help us realign our path with His will. In studying the Bible, I found God's fairness, mercy, and justice demonstrated in the scriptures below:

- **Deuteronomy 32:4:** *He is the Rock, his work is perfect: for all his ways are judgment: a God of truth and without iniquity, just and right is He.*

This verse affirms that God's ways are perfect and just. He is a God of truth and fairness.

- **Psalm 25:8-9:** *Good and upright is the Lord: therefore will He teach sinners in the way. The meek will He guide in judgment: and the meek will He teach His way.*

God's goodness and upright nature ensure that He guides us with fairness and teaches us His ways.

- **Psalm 89:14:** *Justice and judgment are the habitation of His throne: mercy and truth shall go before His face.*

God's throne is founded on justice and judgment, and He governs with mercy and truth.

- **Isaiah 30:18:** *And therefore will the Lord wait, that He may be gracious unto you, and therefore will He be exalted, that He may have mercy upon you: for the Lord is a God of judgment: blessed are all they that wait for Him.*

This verse highlights God's patience and mercy, underscoring His just nature.

❧ **Micah 6:8:** *He hath shewed thee, O man, what is good; and what doth the Lord require of thee, but to do justly, and to love mercy, and to walk humbly with thy God?*

God calls us to live justly and love mercy, reflecting His own fair and just nature.

❧ **Romans 2:6-7:** *Who will render to every man according to his deeds: To them who by patient continuance in well doing seek for glory and honor and immortality, eternal life.*

God's fairness is evident in His promise to reward each person according to their deeds.

❧ **James 1:7:** *Every good gift and every perfect gift is from above, and cometh down from the Father of lights, with whom is no variableness, neither shadow of turning.*

God's unwavering fairness is demonstrated by His consistent and perfect gifts. Regardless of what happens in your life, in spite of who comes and who goes, I encourage you to never stop trusting God. Never stop believing His Word. Don't become immersed in grief, absorbed in pain, or caught up in hard times. God is bigger than everything and anything that you could ever face. My life is a testimony that God is good. He is faithful. He is Just. He is Fair. He is Kind and He is Loving. I survived what I believed to be one of the worst seasons of my life because I kept moving forward. I did it through prayers, tears, and counseling. I was blessed to be surrounded by those whom God orchestrated to go through that season with me. I'm reminded of the time when my grandfather was teaching me to drive. It was pouring down raining and I couldn't see anything. I wanted us to pull over, but my grandfather said, *"Puff you have got to keep going. Sooner or later, the rain is going to stop."* I learned that if you stop in the middle of the storm, there is no telling what danger you will encounter but if you keep going, you will look back and realize that God is fair, and you have the victory.

Some started with me but didn't stay to see me through. Others started with me and are still standing like strong oak trees. I am grateful for them all. As a woman of God, I am growing and continuing to learn. At the time of this writing, I am two years divorced and I still have my moments, but they don't hurt like they used to. God is restoring me, even now as I write. All things have, will and are working for my good. The half of my life has not been told. You can make it beloved. You will make it beloved.

Lessons Learned:

- ✎ There are times in life when you have to grieve the loss of your expectations falling apart and still have the courage to look towards the future and believe again.

- Divorce is hard; having to endure the loss of something or someone valuable to you, is hard; grieving is hard as well.

- Regardless of what happens in your life, in spite of who comes and who goes, I encourage you to never stop trusting God.

- I kept moving forward. I did it through prayers, tears, and counseling. I was blessed to be surrounded by those whom God orchestrated to go through that season with me.

My Thoughts

Venisha Terrae Jackson

 Venisha Terrae Jackson was born and raised in Rochester, New York. In 2007, she relocated to Little Rock, Arkansas. While there, she was employed with Little Rock School District. Wanting a fresh start, Venisha relocated again in 2023 to Houston, Texas. She currently is employed with Humble ISD. Venisha enjoys spending time with family and friends, traveling and journaling. She is the Godmother to Karter B, Lauryn, Konnor and Tre whom she loves and cherishes dearly. She is the author of Lessons From Divorce: From Tragedy to Triumph.